Speak a Powerful Magic

Speak a Powerful Magic

Ten Years of the Traveling Stanzas Poetry Project

Wick Poetry Center

Foreword by Naomi Shihab Nye

Published in association with Chautauqua Institution

Black Squirrel Books® Kent, Ohio

This publication was made possible in part through the generous support of

The Thomas and Mimi Freeman Family Fund

A portion of the proceeds from the sale of this book will support the Traveling Stanzas project and our continued outreach with Chatauqua Institution.

BLACK SQUIRREL BOOKS® 🐿®

Frisky, industrious black squirrels are a familiar sight on the Kent State University campus and the inspiration for Black Squirrel Books®, a trade imprint of The Kent State University Press. www.KentStateUniversityPress.com.

Contents

Foreword

NAOMI SHIHAB NYE

"... don't forget to pause and find a pocket of time to rest inside a stanza, the little room of a poem."—David Hassler

A traveler needs resting spots. A daily regular human being at home needs resting moments. Roadside stops, benches, lobbies, a small coffee shop in which to lay your burdens down. We are all travelers, one kind or another—on some days the trip from bedroom to kitchen to mailbox to grocery might feel like a big journey. The trip through loss, the journey into remembrance . . .

When I think of so many people in our shared world fleeing desperate situations, with little comforts or road snacks of any kind, and no assurance of what waits on the other end of the road—I realize how complacent we've become—the ones who travel with tickets and bags. We rarely consider how graced we are. We note how late our flight is. Our backs hurt, we're so hungry.

How easy is it to observe one another from such conditions? How easy to remember the ones we can't even see?

Poetry helps us know one another quickly, offers intimate insight, encourages us to remember and imagine. With the tiniest line or phrase, a whole mood can change. Language feels real again. Other human beings with their own thoughts surround us. A poem is thin enough to be slipped into the outer pocket of a suitcase or jacket. It won't weigh you down, but it might lift you up.

Speak a Powerful Magic is an act of pure love, from start to finish.

The voices it contains are heartening, humane.

Many of the poems in *Speak a Powerful Magic* contain lines that have accompanied me on my own travels for years. I carried Rita Dove's "… luck leaked out of everywhere" to Dubai and Doha, stood it on the table next to the lamp by the bed. Maj Ragain's "Our work is to listen harder" reminded me what I was doing in Hong Kong and Tokyo. Ella Hassler's "I have been thinking about living like a circle" helped me apprehend the rhythms of days when any traveler feels both energetic and exhausted. The Akron 4th graders, "I hear the world sing / and my voice / SINGS BACK" gave me my traveling anthem to tiny towns in Wyoming and Maine. All of us need companions on our roads—so we won't feel too lonely—so we might remember whatever gave us hope to begin with. The powerful, very magical voices of these wondrous traveling stanzas carry the contagion of possibility—this is what someone said! Now what will you say? It's a pass-it-on magic. Finally, after so much travel and hard work, these beautiful poems will live together in a comfortable book to serve even more of us.

There are so many things to love about the Traveling Stanzas project—its inclusiveness—poems by 3rd graders pressed right up against internationally known voices, elders, immigrants. Juan Felipe Herrera! Maggie Anderson! We're all poets together—each poem honored with equal attention of presentation. A huge part of the joyous endeavor is the gripping artwork, utilizing brilliant images from the visual communication design students at Kent State University. So many topics, details, scenes shine through the poems—Traveling Stanzas feels like real life, as interesting as the days we hope to live all the time. This project's great website (https://travelingstanzas.com) has to be one of the most joyous websites ever created.

Speak a Powerful Magic makes us feel part of a larger family of friends and reminds us there are so many more members of community out there everywhere, searching for words, trying to speak, shaping the lines. If you use these poems as examples in classrooms, they will never fail to ignite further voices, more lines. Couple them with other poems you love and you have an entire syllabus to share. When Addyson Urban says, "I want to inch my way across life," I fall back in love with slow, patient effort. When the students of Jamestown High School encourage us to "find the poem in the world," I know we can never be too lost for very long. Thank you, Wick Poetry Center, David Hassler, and all the poets you reach, for your passionate work of encouraging and collecting and presenting, and for giving us all so many homes.

Acknowledgments

Founded in 1984 by Bob and Walter Wick in memory of their sons Stan and Tom, the Wick Poetry Center at Kent State University promotes opportunities for emerging and established poets and poetry audiences locally, regionally, and nationally. We are grateful for the support and generosity of the Wick family. We also wish to thank the Thomas and Mimi Freeman Family Fund for its support of this publication.

Since 2009, the Traveling Stanzas project has received generous support from the John S. and James L. Knight Foundation, The Burbick Foundation, Woodward Foundation, Hometown Bank, and the Ohio Arts Council. Additionally, we are grateful for the support of our partners: Chautauqua Institution, Portage Medical Center Foundation at UH Portage Medical Center, the City of Kent, Main Street Kent, Kent Free Library, Kent State University Libraries, Kent State University School of Nursing, Conservancy for the Cuyahoga Valley National Park, March for Science, Akron Public Schools, International Institute of Akron, Project Learn, Urban Vision, Akron Children's Hospital, Summa Foundation, Cleveland Clinic Lerner College of Medicine of Case Western Reserve University, Inamori International Center for Ethics and Excellence at Case Western Reserve University, Akron Metro, PARTA, and Western Reserve Public Media.

Among the many individuals who have generously contributed to the project, we would like to especially thank Cathy Hemming and Carol W. Gould.

We are grateful for the ongoing support of the College of Arts and Sciences and our partnership with the School of Visual Communication Design and the College of Communication and Information, as well as our ongoing work with Each + Every in Kent. We are very thankful to The Kent State University Press for their belief in this project; in particular, we wish to thank the director of the Press, Susan

Wadsworth-Booth, assistant editor Katherine Saunders, and designer Christine Brooks. The Traveling Stanzas project continues to flourish thanks to the dedicated work of all staff members of the Wick Poetry Center, past and present, including Maggie Anderson, David Hassler, Jessica Jewell, Györgyi Mihályi-Jewell, Charles Malone, and Nicole Robinson, and dedicated VCD professors Valora Renicker, Christopher Darling, Andrew Fogle, Daphne Peters, and Doug Goldsmith.

We would like to dedicate this book in loving memory of two beloved Kent State professors and community leaders: poet Maj Ragain and illustrator Christopher Darling.

Introduction

DAVID HASSLER
Director, Wick Poetry Center

At the Wick Poetry Center, we believe that all of us, young and old, published writers or not, have the capacity to give voice to our lives, to spark new meaning through the memorable language and leaping thought of a poem, and to share it with others. We believe that poetry can build bridges between the familiar and the unfamiliar and be the means by which we come to know ourselves.

Speak a Powerful Magic is built upon this belief.

In 2009, the Wick Poetry Center was invited by Valora Renicker, Associate Professor of Visual Communication Design, to collaborate with her visual communication design students to create illustrations in response to curated poems from the community. Though the Traveling Stanzas project has grown significantly in mission and scope in the last decade, our partnership with Kent State visual communication design students continues today, while we have also engaged other students and alumni to create designs for specific occasions or projects. Traveling Stanzas illustrations have been displayed on regional and national mass transit, interactive media, and in galleries and community spaces around the world. This book now brings together more than 50 Traveling Stanzas poetry illustrations in celebration of the project's tenth anniversary.

The mission of Traveling Stanzas is simple: to bring poetry to everyday lives so that we may encounter a poem where we may not expect to find it—"published" in public spaces rather than in the pages of a book, wrapped around a metal utility box or installed on an outdoor kiosk, displayed as a mural on a lobby wall, above commuters' heads on mass transit trains and buses, on coffee shop and library walls, or shared as a greeting card or digital media on our interactive website. Coupled with striking, colorful illustrations, these public installations invite all of us, and particularly those who might not normally read a poem or pick up a poetry book, to pause and reflect on our lives, to feel renewed or inspired, and to connect with others through a shared, creative expression.

Over the last ten years of Traveling Stanzas, we have furthered our mission by offering writing workshops in schools, healthcare facilities, literacy centers, libraries, national parks, social service agencies for refugee and immigrant populations, senior centers, and veterans' organizations. By establishing programs with veterans, with caregivers, and in medical settings with patients, the Wick Poetry Center has been able to focus workshops to inspire healing. The Old English verb "to heal" means to make whole. These poems have offered ways for participants to make sense of their condition or their memories, to heal even when there is no cure, and to integrate this knowledge with the larger story of their lives—to create what Anatole Broyard calls "the poem of diagnosis." "Even though I have a hole in my heart from my mom," wrote one participant after a workshop, "the air around it is healing now."

While enrolled in our "Teaching Poetry in the Schools" course, Kent State student poets continue to lead writing workshops in area classrooms. These college students inspire the K–12 students with their lessons that then model a way for younger students to connect with their own passions and motivations, to discover not the "how" but the "why" of their education. Poetry often helps students find a voice, especially those who feel they have not had a voice in class.

In yet another program, our teaching artists use poetry to help English Language Learning (ELL) students—adult and child refugees and immigrants—expand their vocabulary and connect language learning to their lives in an emotional and meaningful way. The Wick Poetry Center developed a method for using English language flash cards, reading aloud a simple model poem that introduces a linguistic pattern and concrete images around a specific subject, such as "Where I'm From," "My Voice," or "My Heart." We then ask participants to speak aloud the word that resonates with them, thereby charging the air with powerful words and images from the model poem. Participants choose several English language flash cards with nouns, adjectives, and verbs, and then use those words to create their own lines. This process encourages participants to play with language and join words in unexpected combinations, sparking new meaning in their poems. In one of these poetry classes, Linda Zhao wrote about the grandmother she had left in China:

I am the compass needle,
and you are the fully magnetic earth
that spins me
to point North.

When she read her poem to the class, she felt the deep listening of the other students who, despite their own mother tongues, recognized themselves in Linda's words. Later she said, "You know, these poems are magic to me."

Speak a Powerful Magic comes out of all these community programs and reminds us that poetry is truly of the people. Alongside poems generated in our community workshops, this book also contains Traveling Stanzas poems from some of the most gifted and famous poets of our time, poets with whom the Wick Poetry Center has engaged through readings and publications.

From wherever poetry arises, we turn to it to give voice to what is troubling us, to honor what we love, to make sense of our lives, to remember our past, and to commemorate what we have lost. From the Italian, "stanza" means a room—a place to pause. Indeed, Traveling Stanzas offers people moments of pause, pockets of time, with which to slow down and reflect on their lives. We invite you to pause in these small rooms and hear the powerful magic of a poem, what poet Li-Young Lee describes as "the inner voice of one person speaking to the inner voice of another."

With major grants from the John S. and James L. Knight Foundation, the Ohio Arts Council, the Burbick Foundation, and the Woodward Foundation, we have been able to enlist the talents of Kent State graphic design students and alumni, which has inspired a cross-cultural, intergenerational conversation through poetry and graphic design. Indeed, the process of pairing these poems with Kent State designers has also brought "happy accidents" and surprises for both the artists and the public. When former US Poet Laureate Juan Felipe Herrera first met the Wick designer Zuzana Kubišová, who illustrated his poem, "My Mother's Name Lucha," he told her he was astonished that the figure and dress Zuzana had drawn reminded him so perfectly of a traditional Mexican dress his mother often wore and a photo of her dancing. When Cleveland resident Jo Steinhurst met with Kent State design student Katie Barnes to talk with her about her poem, "Flags are Flying," they had a rich conversation across generations and life experiences, a conversation between image and word. Jo explained to Katie the tradition of displaying gold stars in the windows of war widows during World War II, and that became the central image of Katie's design for the poem. A year later Jo's niece, Jean Steinhurst Paul, who belongs to the American WWII War Orphan Network, carried posters of that poem translated into French to Drauguinon, France, and the annual ceremony at the Rhone American Cemetery where she presented copies to the mayors of Drauguinon and Doizieux. "Each time I presented the poem," she said, "conversation turned to the great wish for peace in the world."

Our Traveling Stanzas have indeed traveled far in the last ten years and have been translated into six languages, facilitating a global conversation through the intimate and inclusive voice of poetry. These poetry posters and interactive displays have been exhibited not only in a multinational war memorial in Lyon, France, but at the Tuscan Anglo-American Festival in Florence, Italy, and a holiday market in Slovakia, as well as at the Ohio Statehouse, the Library of Congress National Book Festival, and the Chautauqua Institution. Through an ongoing partnership with Chautauqua Literary Arts, the Wick Poetry Center will continue to offer writing workshops in Chautauqua County schools and to promote the voices of those students in our interactive Traveling Stanzas exhibit on the grounds of Chautauqua each summer.

At age six, my daughter said to me one day, while we were walking to school and she was looking up at the trees and the sky, "Daddy, there's a word and a name for everything. Who came up with these names? Where do they come from?" I didn't have an answer for her. Nobody, of course, owns language, and in our own participation as makers of poems, we democratize voice. But it was her question that mattered, her sense of awe and wonder. Our world may appear already to be named, but it is our job as poets and everyday citizens to speak up and rename our sense of belonging in the world. At Holden Elementary School in Kent, Ohio, 3rd-grade student Manasvi Bantawa wrote a poem, "A Tree is Everything," about her favorite tree in her yard, which she called her "childhood friend." In her poem she said, "Tree, you are a big temple for birds." In saying this, she magically renamed that tree and her relationship to it. A poem can be a magic container, a "word temple," or as Donald Hall put it, the "unsayable said."

The poet Stanley Kunitz, in his nineties, wrote, "He who has forgotten the child he was is already too old for poetry." It is easy to lose that sense of curiosity, awe, and wonder that we have as children. Poetry can speak to parts of ourselves that are otherwise untouched or difficult to access. So long as we continue to be in conversation with the children we were, we are never too old, or too young, for poetry. Whether we are an eight-year-old student or a beloved poet in his nineties, we all have the capacity for the leaping thought of poetry, to rub two words together and make a spark—to speak a powerful magic.

The Traveling Stanzas

ODE TO JOY

by Kate Walley's 3rd Grade Class
Seville Intermediate School, Seville, Ohio
Design by Josh Kruszyski, KSU Visual Communication Design student

Oh, *perfect*
POUNCING, PURPLE
JOY

how good to be with you again!

LET US
SING

the pianissimo of the stars
until we beat

as one.

—Kate Walley's 3rd Grade Class

IF I WERE

by Nadia Anwaar
6th Grade, Mrs. Deng's Class, Jennings School, Akron, Ohio
Design by Tori Russell, KSU Visual Communication Design student

If I Were

If I were a flower,
I would sprinkle my colors
to a black and white world,
like makeup to a woman
who just woke up.

If I were a snowflake,
I would dive into the earth
and cover it with my coldness.

If I were a woman,
I would let people see through me
to tell them how beautiful
this world is.

—Nadia Anwaar

PESCADERO

by Mark Doty
Design by Macklin Legan, KSU Visual Communication Design student

The little goats like my mouth and fingers,

and one stands up against the wire fence, and taps on the fence board

a hoof made blacker by the dirt of the field,

pushes her mouth forward to my mouth,

so that I can see the smallish squared seeds of her teeth, and the bristle–whiskers,

and then she kisses me, though I know it doesn't mean "kiss,"

then leans her head way back, arcing her spine, goat yoga,

all pleasure and greeting and then good–natured indifference: She loves me,

she likes me a lot, she takes interest in me, she doesn't know me at all

or need to, having thus acknowledged me. Though I am all happiness,

since I have been welcomed by the field's small envoy, and the splayed hoof,

fragrant with soil, has rested on the fence board beside my hand.

PESCADERO

—Mark Doty

MY VOICE

by Hai Ni Paw Soe
Karen People, displaced from Myanmar
3rd Grade, Urban Vision, Akron, Ohio
Design by Tong Zhao, KSU Visual Communication Design graduate student

My Voice

My voice is a bird
that tweets and sings.
It flies from branch to branch.

My voice follows the moon
and makes me follow my dream.

My voice lives
in a rainbow-colored umbrella.

—Hai Ni Paw Soe

FLAGS ARE FLYING

by Jo Steinhurst, age 86
Judson Manor, Cleveland, Ohio
Design by Katie Barnes, KSU Visual Communication Design student

Flags
are
Flying

Today, flags are flying
outside my window, Fourth of July,
and I am back in my parents' home,
Boston, 1944.

Flags were flying then –
not all red, white and blue,
but white ones, too,
with gold stars
to signify broken hearts.

I remember when the telegram arrived,
just a piece of paper carrying tears
for a wife, a fatherless child,
parents in shock.

Now, more than sixty years
later, no telegram arrives,
yet feelings remain
for wasted lives
untimely end.
While, once again,
flags are flying.

—Jo Steinhurst

LADDER TO THE STARS

by Ella Hassler
6th Grade, Miller South School for the Visual and Performing Arts, Akron, Ohio
Design by Zuzana Kubišová, Wick Designer

Ladder to the stars

I have been thinking,
listening to my heart beat
in rhythm with my soul,
my mind in unison with my toes –
the tap, tap of my stomach
in Morse code.

I have been thinking
about living like a tree,
my arms adorned
with green glass drops.

I have been thinking
about living like a river,
never ending, never stopping,
always rushing, my waters
a looking glass.

I have been thinking
about living like a circle,
a round, perfect circle
like the earth.

I have been thinking,
listening to the planets rumble,
about the Big Bang.
I want to live the Big Bang.
Will it happen again when I die?

I have been thinking,
watching the sunset,
the dark cloth of the sky lifted,
my ribcage a ladder to the stars.

—Ella Hassler

A TREE IS EVERYTHING

by Manasvi Bantawa
3rd Grade, Holden Elementary School, Kent, Ohio
Design by Zack Motrunecs, KSU Visual Communication Design student

A Tree is Everything

a tree is a landmark for the seasons
a big temple for birds
every leaf on the tree crumbles up
on every wave
a drop of rain comes to this world and melts
it is a kiss and a hug
from above and beyond

tree, you have been brave in the snow
you have been strong in the light
you were there in the heavy rain
there in the heavy thunder
tree you are brave and strong
and big like the earth

you are a childhood friend

—Manasvi Bantawa

WHERE I'M FROM

by Elvidio Bufalini, age 88
Judson Manor, Cleveland, Ohio
Design by Lindsay Alberts, KSU Visual Communication Design student

WHERE I'M FROM

I dare say
I am from
 a cherished memory
and the immediacy
 of an intimate moment
harking back
 to the heart's thirsty infancy,
me at the time
 a compliant toddler
sitting content on Grandpa's knee,
 held close in a warm embrace.
 Grandpa's soft white beard
 caresses my quickened face,

the imprinted glow and flow
of his full-grown male affection,
 mothering and fathering me,
 perhaps, in a subtle way,
 through the alchemy
 of fellow-feeling,
nurturing into being
this now-concluding,
 love-blessed life
of an aging man.

—Elvidio Bufalini

THIS PENCIL

by Hei Nay Tha
3rd Grade, Urban Vision, Akron, Ohio
Design by Brandon Mahone, KSU Visual Communication Design student

This Pencil

This pencil is a rope
that pulls my heart and brain
onto the paper.
This pencil is a ladder
I climb to heaven.
This pencil is a branch
that spreads love to the world,
like apples falling down.
This pencil is a wand
sparkling letters
onto the page.

—Hei Nay Tha

MOON IN THE WINDOW

by Dorianne Laux
Design by Alison Farone, KSU Visual Communication Design student

Moon in the Window

I wish I could say I was the kind of child
who watched the moon from her window,
would turn toward it and wonder.
I never wondered. I read. Dark signs
that crawled toward the edge of the page.
It took me years to grow a heart
from paper and glue. All I had
was a flashlight, bright as the moon,
a white hole blazing beneath the sheets.

—Dorianne Laux

MY VOICE

by Lesli Smith and Kathleen Collins's Project Learn GED Class, Akron, Ohio
Design by Nick Blanchard, KSU Visual Communication Design student

MY VOICE

My voice lives in my grandmother's apple pie

It is soothing
It is soft
It is brilliant

My voice is a lullaby

It smells like morning after a fresh rain

My voice cries
from my childhood

It washes away evil

My voice is swimming
Keeping pace

scoop kick
breathe
scoop kick
breathe

My voice comes from the deep

—Lesli Smith and Kathleen
Collins's Project Learn GED class

REFUGE

by Adam Khan
5th Grade, Wick Juniors Writing Club, Kent, Ohio
Design by Zuzana Kubišová, Wick Designer

Refuge

A book is refuge,
a friend I can talk to,
a home away from home.

A book is a doorway
to imagination, every page
a rushing river of words.

I read to see the world
from a different perspective,
to hide away in a secret corner
and create peace.
I read to carry on the story.

— Adam Khan

DRIVING WHILE BLACK

by Mwatabu S. Okantah
Design by Zuzana Kubišová, Wick Designer

driving while black

It is not what you call me,
it is what i answer to…
        —African Proverb

driving in my car
black wisdom from the ages is turned on its head:

in my car
what i think of my Self is of no significance
(save in my own mind…)
because i am always black while driving
and i know *they* are there   waiting   lurking
looking
out for some one black
like me.

i am a black man driving.
i have my own and countless other *blackmenintheircars*
stories to tell—
it is the same story; just new chapters from works in
progress
out of America's deep black story well.

i am blessed.
i have driven through my youth
and into my elder years—
i am still driving. *they are*
still there watching.
sadly,
their fears are always near…

—Mwatabu S. Okantah

FINDING THE POEM IN THE WORLD

by Mrs. Price and Mrs. Rowe-Baehr's students
Jamestown High School, Jamestown, New York
In partnership with Chautauqua Institution
Design by Zuzana Kubišová, Wick Designer

Finding the Poem in the World

You may think poems live in a dusty old book,
but they are walking all around us,
daring us to think harder, speak louder.
You can find a poem under moss-covered rocks
along the **Chadakoin River**
or in children rolling with laughter
down the slide at **Bergman Park**.
Poems live in the dainty lace curtains
adorning the windows in **Room 103**
and in the bell that never rings
in front of **Jamestown High School**.
Poems live in the prints of young artists
showcased in the alleys of our **Red Raider's town**,
under the grates on **Third Street**, catching
the secrets of passersby, and in the waves
rolling against the shores of **Chautauqua Lake**.
Poems live in my body, making my toes curl,
fingers tingle, and eyebrows raise.
They live in my dark brown eyes.
My tears are diamonds, and every day I make my poem rich.
Poems live in the vibrations of the world,
stretching out to everyone and everything.
Like the first drop of rain on black pavement,
poems sizzle and evaporate off my tongue.

— Mrs. Price and Mrs. Rowe-Baehr's students

MY VOICE

by Lori Galambos's 4th Grade Class
Miller South School for the Visual and Performing Arts, Akron, Ohio
Design by Ruth Turner, KSU Visual Communication Design student

MY VOICE

MY VOICE FILLS THE AIR WITH SONG
IT POPS OUT LIKE A PURPLE CROCUS IN SPRING
BLOOMING LOUDER EVERY DAY.
MY VOICE CARRIES A SECRET
THEN PASSES IT ON
MY VOICE IS LIKE
AN OVEN — IT DINGS
WHEN A GOOD IDEA IS DONE
MY VOICE MOVES
TO THE VIBRATIONS
OF PEACE
I HEAR THE WORLD SING
AND MY VOICE
SINGS BACK.
—LORI GALAMBOS'S 4TH GRADE CLASS

MILLER SOUTH SCHOOL   AKRON, OHIO

ODE TO MY BODY

by Scott Parsons's 12th Grade Class
Maplewood Career Center, Ravenna, Ohio
Design by Erin Stearns, KSU Visual Communication Design student

Bless the ear
   a gateway for laughter
Bless the eyebrow
   bushy with wisdom
Bless the foot
   which gives equilibrium
   to an unstable world
Bless the wrist
   articulate as a spider
Bless the heart
   how it beats even when broken
Bless the mouth
   and its ocean of words
Bless the chest
   the loudest drum of all
Bless the bellybutton
   which is the scar of love.

Ode to My Body
—Scott Parsons's 12th Grade Class

HEALING HANDS

by Palliative Care Team
Summa Health System, Akron, Ohio
Design by Ian McCullough, KSU Visual Communication Design student

HEALING
HANDS

MY HANDS THAT DELIVERED BABIES,
PATTED THEIR TENDER FEET,
NOW CRADLE THE DYING AND BEREAVED,
BEAR WITNESS TO FINAL SACRED BREATHS.
TIRED AND CRACKED,
WASHED AND SCRUBBED,

MY HANDS RESTORE MEMORIES,
SOOTHE AND CALM.
THEY WIPE AWAY A TEAR
AND BURST FORTH IN SONG.
MY HEART HAS TAUGHT MY HANDS
TO FOLD IN PRAYER
AND OPEN TO GRACE.

— PALLIATIVE CARE TEAM
SUNNIA HEALTH SYSTEM

MY MOTHER'S NAME LUCHA

by Juan Felipe Herrera
Design by Zuzana Kubišová, Wick Designer

Overleaf
SOME DAYS

by Kent State University College of Nursing faculty, students, and alumni
Created in Healing Stanzas Writing Workshops facilitated by the Wick Poetry Center
Design by Each + Every

My Mother's Name Lucha

your hands my hands
kindnesses dances silences sitting   you i
          El Paso Texas Segundo Barrio
Juarez 1918   1936 in gypsy   dress actress
you sing   i sing we sing   lullabies of old
this   now lines now   my birth
heart now life

                              all life   now
              i   bow   to you

— Juan Felipe Herrera

S O M A D

*In Celebration of the
College of Nursing
50th Anniversary*

SOME DAYS you'll wake up
and know
your life has a purpose
This is who you are
who you want to be
a nurse

Your arms will open like doors
welcoming those in need
You do not know all the stories
but you will learn to become them

Some days you'll feel a fire in your chest
as if the whole world is burning
You'll feel your tongue fold inward
the weight of unspoken words
flutters in your stomach
and clogs in your throat

Some days your heart will crumble like crust
and when the beeping stops
you will feel in your nostrils
a burning void

Some days all the lines and scribbles
of your life
will make a picture
You'll feel like being a daisy
though everyone around you
wants you to be a rose

Never forget nature's healing touch
or the comfort
of a wrinkled hand
          reaching out to you

Some days your heart will feel
heavy with hope
You'll wipe away the worries
and the why me's
and realize hurt
and healing
          are not so different

Some days you'll reach for the stars
          wishing you had longer arms
you'll break into a million pieces
          and call yourself confetti
or look at another and feel
          for just that moment
          everything is right with the world

E

Your mouth can speak
          a powerful magic
Your heart is
          a lighthouse in your body
Remember your patients can teach you lessons
          greater than any you will hear
          in a lecture hall.

Some days with grace and grit,
you'll know the work of a nurse
is the work of the heart
sacred and profane

Find your passion
          let it write your story
This is who you are
          who you want to be
          a nurse

Y

S

This collaborative poem was created
by Kent State University's College
of Nursing faculty, students, and
alumnae during Healing Stanzas
writing workshops, conducted in
2017 by the Wick Poetry Center.
Edited by David Hassler

MY GRANDMA

by Ágnes Haiszer-Silling, Hungary
International Institute of Akron and Project Learn
Design by Vanessa Okojie, KSU graduate student

My Grandma

whose arms are a safe, warm coat
in the ice cold winter

whose laughter is like the sound
of trickling streams

who smells like a freshly baked cake

whose hair is whiter than the snow

who takes care of her family
like a giant tree

whose branches give shelter
to a lone wanderer in a storm

whose love is stronger than
a fortress wall.

—Ágnes Haiszer-Silling

SOLDIER'S HEART

by Maj Ragain
Design by David Steckel, KSU Visual Communication Design student

Soldier's Heart
—for The Warrior's Journey Home Veterans' Healing Circle

We sing the old wounds,
word by word, stitch by stitch,

many hands, many voices.
The needle hurts as the thread

is drawn through, the mouth
of the wound drawn shut.

Our work is to listen hard,
to look the wounded in the eye,

to stitch and pull
press through pain,

until every knot is tied,
every last wound closed,

every broken heart
healed and whole.

— Maj Ragain

"All nurturing begins with inclusion" — Roshi Robert Aitken

MY HEART

by Farid Ahmad Alkozai, Afghanistan
International Institute of Akron and Project Learn
Design by Zuzana Kubišová, Wick Designer

My Heart

My heart is a letter.
Every time it is sent to someone
they tear the envelope.

My heart is a glass.
When I am thirsty the glass is empty
with no water.

My heart is a phone.
When I want to call someone
it doesn't have the charge.

My heart is a door.
After work,
when I come to my house,

the door is locked.

– Farid Ahmad Alkozai

TESTIMONIAL

by Rita Dove

Design by Christopher Darling (1981–2018), Assistant Professor,
   KSU Visual Communication Design

TESTIMONIAL

Back when the earth was new
and heaven just a whisper,
back when the names of things
hadn't had time to stick;

back when the smallest breezes
melted summer into autumn;
when all the poplars quivered
sweetly in rank and file...

the world called, and I answered.
Each glance ignited to a gaze.
I caught my breath and called that life,
swooned between spoonfuls of lemon sorbet.

I was pirouette and flourish,
I was filigree and flame.
How could I count my blessings
when i didn't know their names?

Back when everything was still to come,
luck leaked out of everywhere.
I gave my promise to the world,
and the world followed me here.

— Rita Dove

YOU & I

by Linda Zhao, China
International Institute of Akron and Project Learn
Design by Alison Farone, KSU Visual Communication Design alumnus

YOU & I

– for my grandmother

I am the growing grass,
and you are the nurturing dew
that kisses my blades in the morning.

I am the underground tunnel,
and you are the famous archaeologist
that discovered me
and brought me out of the dark.

I am the compass needle,
and you are the fully magnetic earth
that spins me
to point North.

–Linda Zhao

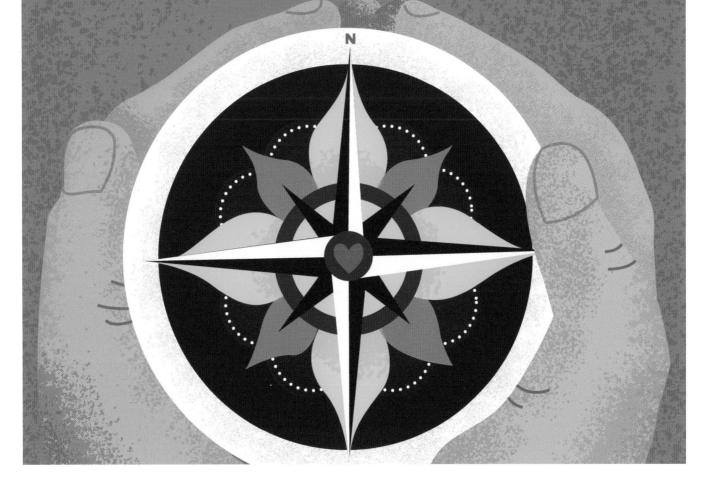

WITH ALL THESE MOMENTS

by Campbell Budzar
5th Grade, Holden Elementary, Kent, Ohio
Design by Joanne Chiu, KSU Visual Communication Design student

With All These Moments

With all these moments
which grew, then
picked, and all those
who shot, snapped, raced, across
this time of floral grace
and those

  forgotten
  left behind
  a level of heart.

And thee, who ripened my moments
then sweetened and baked
as tender enough to eat
and those who greatened our moments
and kneaded our bread

  and made such a
  such a...
  Difference

—Campbell Budzar

THANK YOU, TREE

by Fatou M'Baye
5th Grade, Holden Elementary School, Kent, Ohio
Design by Alex Catanese, KSU Visual Communication Design alumnus

THANK YOU, TREE

—

Tree, you put the spark
back in my body.
And when I take a breath,
the lights behind my eyes
are turned on, and the fire
in my furnace crackles.
The whole world stops buzzing.

For once the Earth
will have a chance to think
and remember why we're here.
On that day, I'll look at you, tree,
through your leaves, your bark,
your sapwood, all the way to your heart—
your beating, beating heart—
and say, "thank you."

—FATOU M'BAYE

MY VOICE

by Danial Javanmard Fasihdel, Iran
International Institute of Akron and Project Learn
Design by Frédéric Vigne, KSU Visual Communication Design student

My voice is water
that washes dirty memories from my mind.

My voice is a pair of shoes
holding my feet on the difficult road ahead.

My voice is an umbrella that protects me
from the backbiting whispers of others.

My voice used to be an ash bin
of lies and deception, but now
it is an open treasure of truth and peace.

—Danial Javanmard Fasihdel

THE NAMES ON THE WALL

by Joe Caley, Vietnam War veteran
Design by Ivan Sugerman, KSU Visual Communication Design student

THE NAMES ON THE WALL

demons of the past
eat my soul
with a full-blown appetite

on foot in the jungle
my heart beats
the only sound

punji pits and underground tunnels
searching all day
finding nothing

what occurred long ago
just happened yesterday
tracing the names on the wall

a warrior's journey to heal
my memories turn to shadows
as if they are etched

on the back of my mind

— Joe Caley

MY HERO

by Billy Collins
Design by Megan Bush, KSU Visual Communication Design student

MY HERO

Just as the hare is zipping across the finish line,

the tortoise has stopped once again

by the roadside,

this time to stick out his neck

and nibble a bit of sweet grass,

unlike the previous time

when he was distracted

by a bee humming in the heart of a wildflower.

—Billy Collins

A WINTER SUNSET

by Ted Kooser
Design by Larrie King, KSU graduate student

a winter sunset

At the foot of the hill,
the trees have pulled on
boots of shadow. Where,
I ask them, do they think
they're going? "Round
the world," they answer,
"back by morning."

—Ted Kooser

INSIDE A WHISPER

by Mason Lewis
4th Grade, Holden Elementary, Kent, Ohio
Design by Bryan Gilligan, KSU Visual Communication Design student

Inside a Whisper

Charge inside a whisper.
That is what I would do –
and bounce from sound to sound,
hearing dodgy, clattery
secrets that swerve
inside and out, and prance
from one atom to another.

Outside a whisper it is quiet,
like butterflies in a field,
while inside, it is a different world,
where creatures slouch and lounge,
hearing secrets so loud,
they have to deliver them
to the next person.

—*Mason Lewis*

FADO

by Jane Hirshfield
Design by Kara Wellman, KSU Visual Communication Design alumnus

FADO

A man reaches close
and lifts a quarter
from inside a girl's ear,
from her hands takes a dove
she didn't know was there.
Which amazes more,
you may wonder:
the quarter's serrated murmur
against the thumb
or the dove's knuckled silence?
That he found them,
or that she never had,
or that in Portugal,
this same half-stopped moment,
it's almost dawn,
and a woman in a wheelchair
is singing a fado
that puts every life in the room
on one pan of a scale,
itself on the other,
and the copper bowls balance.

—Jane Hirshfield

MY SOUL

by Hsa Ehser Byu
Karen People, displaced from Myanmar
6th grade, Urban Vision, Akron, Ohio
Design by Jenna Myler, KSU Visual Communication Design student

My Soul

My soul follows the echo

of my dreams.

My soul is a jar full of secrets.

My soul is a bright light

high in the galaxies of my eyes.

My soul pushes and pulls.

It guides me away from trouble.

— Hsa Ehser Byu

INCHWORM

by Addyson Urban
3rd Grade, Longcoy Elementary, Kent, Ohio
Design by Zuzana Kubišová, Wick Designer

Inchworm

want to inch my way across life.
It will take a long time,

but I don't care.

I will celebrate the long journey.
I want to inch across town

and look at all the things I can
before

the sun
sets.

—Addyson Urban

DEAR MONARCH

by Mrs. Vesia's Preschool Class
KSU Child Development Center
Design by Alison Farone, KSU Visual Communication Design alumnus

Dear Monarch

A caterpillar is so big,
so why are your wings so small?
Who painted your wings orange?
Fairies? Did they paint you all colors?

Your wings are pointed
and spotted, as if they're shouting,
"You can't eat me!"
to your predators.

What do you do inside your chrysalis?
Do you drink milk?
Do you sit on a little couch
with teeny pillows?

You get cold in the winter,
since you don't have a tiny coat or boots.
So you spread your wings
like a superhero and fly to Mexico.

When you get there,
do you fold your wings
to make a dress
and go dancing?

—Mrs. Vesia's Preschool Class

MY GRANDFATHER

by Luwela Esube
Democratic Republic of the Congo
International Institute of Akron and Project Learn
Design by Zuzana Kubišová, Wick Designer

My Grandfather

whose stories were large
like a tree's shadow
under which many people
could rest
who walked slowly like a turtle
reflecting kindness
who was over one hundred
and like a precious suitcase
contained wealthy things
whose heart was open
like a flower
on which bees could land
to collect pollen
whose voice was like honey
my grandfather
whose life is a mirror to me

– Luwela Esube

DRIVING

by Kate Daniels
Design by Zuzana Kubišová, Wick Designer

That was the year that summer lingered

and fall came on late. I was still wearing

sleeveless clothes when the temperatures fell,

and the wind rose suddenly, and tore the leaves

from their branches in a matter of days.

By then, there was a long line of addicts

on the corner every morning — red–nosed

and shivering, sores all over, reminding me

of the roaming packs of starving dogs you see

in third world countries. I shooed them away

when they begged for money... All that autumn,

DRIVING

I was searching for my son. Why I never looked

among the junkies on the corner who, after all,

were other people's sons, or why — god help me —

I drove right through their tattered clots,

and kept my coins to myself, and controlled

my thoughts — I have no clue. I just kept driving

though I had no sense of where I was going,

or what I'd do, or what I might find if I got there.

—Kate Daniels

SUPERHERO

by Day Soe Wah
Karen People, displaced from Myanmar
5th Grade, Urban Vision, Akron, Ohio
Design by Lisa Cook, KSU Visual Communication Design graduate student

SUPERHERO

My superhero can't save all lives.
My superhero can't dodge bullets or knives.
My superhero can't fight bad people.
My superhero can't fight against evil.
My superhero does not have any powers.
My superhero can't fly over towers.

BUT WHAT HE CAN DO IS LOVE ME.

He can work hard and do his job for me.

MY SUPERHERO IS MY DAD.

— Day Soe Wah

WHY I WRITE

by Scott Parsons's Writing Community Classes
Hathaway Brown School's Osborne Writing Center, Shaker Heights, Ohio
Design by Bridget Elchert, KSU Visual Communication Design student

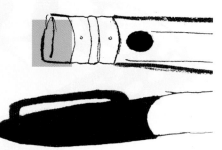

Why I Write

I write because the feel of paper
under my pencil is always the same,
though the friction of words is different.

I write to see a reflection
besides the one in my mirror.

I write, waving a butterfly net
through the garden,
to catch my childhood before it escapes.
I write to hold on. I write to let go.

I write because it hurts,
because even if the poem falls apart,
the hollow where it could have been,
the impact of its absence,
like water shaping the shore,

is still there.

—Scott Parsons's Writing Community
Classes, Hathaway Brown
School's Osborne Writing Center

MY SOUL

by Desman Tucker
6th Grade, Urban Vision, Akron, Ohio
Design by Allison Durant, KSU Visual Communication Design student

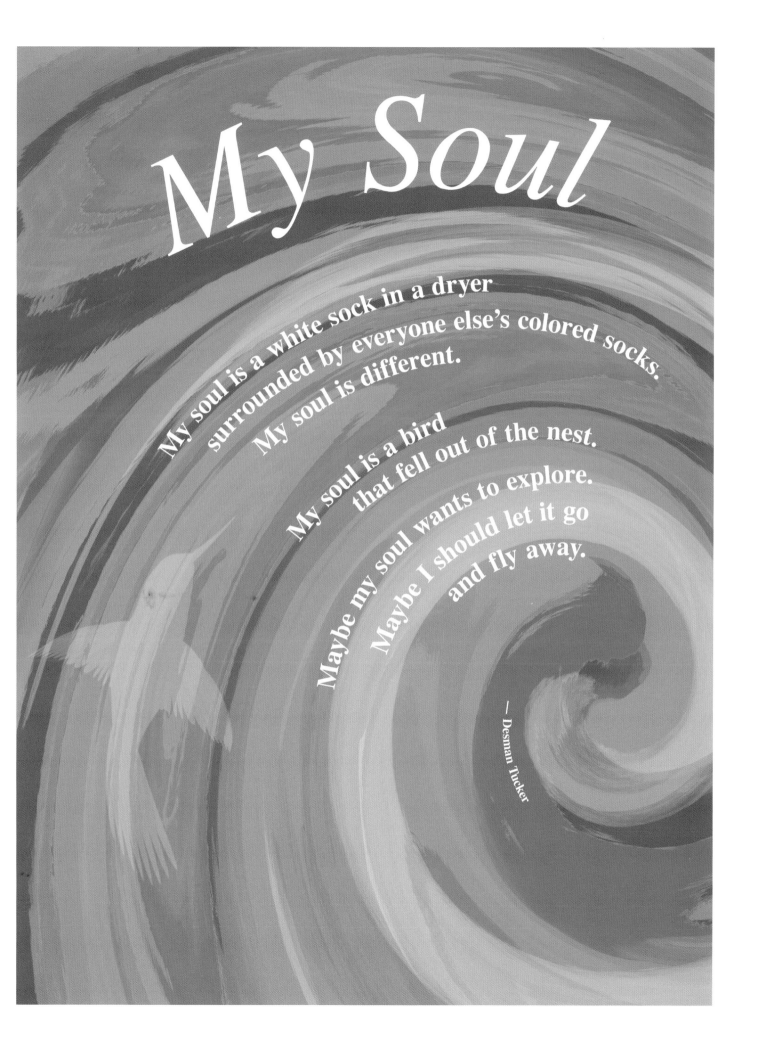

My Soul

My soul is a white sock in a dryer
surrounded by everyone else's colored socks.
My soul is different.

My soul is a bird
that fell out of the nest.
Maybe my soul wants to explore.
Maybe I should let it go
and fly away.

— Desman Tucker

HOW THE BRAIN WORKS

by Maggie Anderson
Design by Zuzana Kubišová, Wick Designer

How the Brain Works

Like a peony. Full white blossoms,
heavy and damp with the scurrying
of insects. From this comes language:
Morning sun. Afternoon shower. This, that.
It gathers to fit in open palms, heart shape
that wants to carry one flower as far
as it has to, as fast as it's able, to the dark
oak table, the red cut-glass bowl.
The ants will drop and crawl to the windowsill.
Soft petals will brown and slime,
fall down to re-enter the earth.
And the brain says, happy.
The brain says, do over, do over.

– Maggie Anderson

ALTAR BOY AT THE GRAND TETONS

by Regis Louis Coustillac
Kent State University undergraduate student
Design by Zuzana Kubišová, Wick Designer

Overleaf
PLEDGE

by Participants of the 2018 March for Science Advocacy Summit, Chicago, Illinois
Created in writing workshops facilitated by the Wick Poetry Center
Design by Each + Every

ALTAR BOY AT THE GRAND TETONS

When did I begin to dance past
the path of broken branches,
so satisfied with wandering lost
beneath an empty barrel of dying stars?

I look up to curse the moon
and see a single comet burn across the night.
It is a blessing on the forehead.
Ash Wednesday.

So I plant myself on a bed of moss,
and glaze my hands with dew and dirt.
A blessing on my forehead.
I begin to pray for rain.

—Regis Louis Coustillac

A BRIGHT LIGHT streams through my window.
I look up to thank the gift of the Sun
whose energy drives our own,
tangled clouds of magnetism blasting from the golden orb.

**I pledge allegiance to the coastline,
the meeting of earth and sea, solid and fluid,
to the depths of the oceans
and the life that remains undiscovered,
curiosities for our wonder.**

Pledge

—MARCH FOR SCIENCE ADVOCACY SUMMIT

I pledge allegiance to the diatoms, carbon fixers,
master architects of glass in our waters,
living snowflakes, swirling, sweeping to infinity.

I pledge allegiance to the ocean, more original than
the origin of species, source of fear and awe,
now suffering herself, polluted.

**I pledge allegiance to the spaces
where we are welcome.
And I pledge to challenge the status quo
in the spaces where we are not.**

I pledge allegiance to soil, home of free-living
nitrogen-fixing bacteria and fungi,
to the raw, crumbly matter holding the capacity for life.

I pledge allegiance to the gothic cathedrals of caves
their columns of dripping stalactites,
the flapping wings of bats,
a choir echoing through ancient corridors.

To trees, tall and green, I pledge allegiance...
To the call of the loon by the lake.
To creeks, with their bubbles and gurgles.

I pledge allegiance
to the starry night sky
washed out by bright city lights,
one Galaxy, in brilliance, above all.

I pledge allegiance to the triple helix,
the interstitial glue holding our cells,
our selves, together.

**I pledge allegiance to resilience
and resistance
to our blind, tenacious spirit,
ever adapting.**

**I pledge allegiance to the prairie,
root mass vining through native soil,
seed head flags waving in the
summer storms.**

I pledge allegiance to my mountain,
always present in my view.
A touchstone, grounding me,
humbling me with its scale.

I pledge allegiance to the endless
details of its mass.
The fern frond, verdant with orange specks.
The shrouded salamander.
The fallen, decaying log returning
to the earth beneath my feet.
I pledge to be guardian of my habitat.

I pledge allegiance to the people in this room
and the potential we represent
for social change,
for justice,
for science in service
for all

WITNESS THE RIVER

by Jake Soyars
7th Grade, Wick Juniors Writing Club, Kent, Ohio
Design by Rachel Slingluff, KSU Visual Communication Design student

Witness The River

Witness the river,
the way it whispers ancient words
spoken by slithering streams
and vast oceans.

Witness the loneliness of the river,
how it longs for you,
but can't quite reach you.

Witness the strange power
flowing through you,
traveling slowly
and brushing against your ankles—
something you can only feel
if you witness the river.

—Jake Soyars

MY MOTHER

by Usama Halak, Syria
International Institute of Akron and Project Learn
Design by Lisa Olszewski, KSU Visual Communication Design student

my mother

Whose eyes were like the surface
    of a quiet sea
Whose words were like pure water
    irrigating thirsty fields
Whose advice gave clarity
    like eyeglasses
    so I could see the right way
My mother whose face
    was like a garden
Every time I looked at her
    I rested among its fragrant flowers

—Usama Halak

VESPERTINA COGNITIO

by Natasha Trethewey
Design by Zuzana Kubišová, Wick Designer

Vespertina Cognitio

Overhead, pelicans glide in threes—
　　their shadows across the sand
　　　　dark thoughts crossing the mind.

Beyond the fringe of coast, shrimpers
　　hoist their nets, weighing the harvest
　　　　against the day's losses. Light waning,

concentration is a lone gull
　　circling what's thrown back. Debris
　　　　weights the trawl like stones.

All day, this dredging—beneath the tug
　　of waves—rhythm of what goes out,
　　　　comes back, comes back, comes back.

— Natasha Trethewey

MY HEART

by Yanqin Weng, China
International Institute of Akron and Project Learn
Design by Zuzana Kubišová, Wick Designer

My Heart

My heart is a box of bright crayons
that can draw my rich imagination
and my multi-colored life.

My heart is like foggy glasses.
I can't see the world as clearly as I would like to.

My heart is like a pair of dancing shoes
that can take my soul to any destination
and spin with the scenery.

My heart is a natural clock.
I wish I could turn its hands back to the past
to spend more time with my mom.

—Yanqin Weng

RECOVERY

by Dustin Kosley
University Hospitals Portage Medical Center
Design by Zuzana Kubišová, Wick Designer

RECOVERY

Recovery is like a caterpillar
evolving into a beautiful creature.
Or like a spider that crawls up
a down spout
and gets knocked back to the begining,
only to continue upward
refusing to give in!

Doors open and a whole new life emerges.
From your past doors close,
letting out light from its cracks,
so it may be remembered.

Recovery is not easy.
It demands discipline and understanding
continuous attention, and reflection.
A requirement of hope.

Recovery needs hard work and strength,
like building a home
with brick and mortar
mending.

Recovery is discovery.
You are an explorer
finding yourself in a new land.

Recovery is one minute, one day,
one week at a time.
It works if you work it.

— Dustin Kosley

THE FIELDS OF CLYMER

by Mrs. Amber Brunco's Classes
Clymer Central School, Clymer, New York
In partnership with Chautauqua Institution
Design by Zuzana Kubišová, Wick Designer

The Fields of Clymer

I am from the backwoods,
from the forest and the mist-clouded mountains,
the mosquitoes that swarm around me.
I am from the coyote's howl at night,
it makes me feel scared and unprotected.
I am from the black stormy valleys of this world.

I am from a big family
bickering, smiles, and love
from the cry of a toddler at 6:30am on a Saturday.
Quiet Sundays in the pews,
long church services filled with prayer and hope.

I am from warm summer days smelling sweet hay
from the Amish horses' feet clicking on the pavement.
I am from the plows hard at work in the fields farmers working before it rains,
from the cow manure that I stomp my boots in.
I am from where your coach is also your history teacher,
from playing basketball in the spotlight,
from getting pulled by the coach.

I am from the gray house on the hill where I took my first steps
and maybe even my final steps.
From the circle of the clock, from the blood in my veins,
the town where everyone knows everyone.
I am from my Dutch roots, May Day and the Tulip Festival,
from New York... "Oh, but not the city."

— Mrs. Amber Brunco's Classes

DURING A WAR

by Naomi Shihab Nye
Design by Branden Vondrak, KSU Visual Communication Design student

During A War

Best wishes to you & yours,
he closes the letter.

For a moment I can't
fold it up again—
where does "yours" end?
Dark eyes pleading

what could we have done
differently?
Your family,
your community,
circle of earth, we did not want,
we tried to stop,
we were not heard

by dark eyes who are dying
now. How easily they
would have welcomed us in
for coffee, serving it
in a simple room
with a radiant rug.
Your friends and mine.

—Naomi Shihab Nye

HOME

by Isabella Rodriguez
2nd Grade, Walls Elementary, Kent, Ohio
Design by Devon Skunta-Helmink, KSU Visual Communication Design student

Home

Suppose there is a city in the Buddha's lap
and his knees are the mountains singing.

Suppose feathers rejoice when they fall
from an eagle's wing, spinning and dancing.

Suppose nature is a map leading to willow trees
where spirits roam, speaking in old voices.

Suppose you can climb rocks like a billy goat
with clanking hooves and horns that curl for battle.

Suppose a path of dandelions and buttercups
takes you back to the mountain,

where you call out, "I'm home."

—Isabella Rodriguez

AMAZING GRACE

by Melissa Soltis, MD
Palliative Care, Summa Health System
Design by Emily Rabatsky, KSU Visual Communication Design student

Amazing Grace

Your daughter sat diligently by your bed
wondering when you would go.

She hovered, the room stale
from frustration, from long days,
exhausting nights, and why
you wouldn't say goodbye.

I asked her to leave,
to get some food:
life, fresh breath.

I knew your song, your favorite hymn,
I sang it to you then.
You inhaled, you exhaled – that new
perfectly crisp air.

— Melissa Soltis

MY VOICE

by Pay Htoo Paw
Karen People, displaced from Myanmar
6th Grade, Urban Vision, Akron, Ohio
Design by Michael Satira, KSU Visual Communication Design student

my voice

My voice is a lamp that shines
   and takes my sadness away

My voice is an umbrella
   to protect me from getting wet

My voice builds up my goal
   until I reach the finish line

My voice is a ladder,
so when God takes my hand
   I will reach out
   and climb to him

– Pay Htoo Paw

MY SOUL

by Brandon Johnson, age 16
Pediatric Palliative Care patient
Akron Children's Hospital, Akron, Ohio
Design by Terran Washington, KSU Visual Communication Design student

My Soul

My soul is a drop of water
bending light into a rainbow

My soul is a flower, a closed box
waiting for someone to find its secrets

My soul is an opera
singing notes no one has ever dreamed before

My soul was pierced through the neck with an arrow
a trach tube, scarlet blood dripping down

My soul is a first-aid kit
hiding my scars –

a missing link
a treasure

—Brandon Johnson

WHY I WRITE

by Too Doh Paw
Karen People, displaced from Myanmar
7th Grade, Urban Vision, Akron, Ohio
Design by Drew Schneider, KSU Visual Communication Design student

Why I Write

I **write** like a hose spraying water
on the grass
helping the world grow.

I **write** until my hands
become tired like bear cubs
and have to hibernate.

I **write**, waiting for someone
to stumble into my world
and enter my life.

—Too Doh Paw

A DREAM

by Abby Rambler
(Based on the speech by Martin Luther King Jr.)
7th Grade, Miller South School for the Visual and Performing Arts, Akron, Ohio
Design by Each + Every

A DREAM

a dream

is a

beautiful symphony

sing

ing

from prodigious hilltops

from

heightening Alleghenies

from

curvaceous slopes

Let

it ring

—ABBY RAMBLER

LONELINESS

by Rick Keller
Participant in Coleman Professional Services "Options" program
Design by Zuzana Kubišová, Wick Designer

Loneliness

Loneliness you are always around
like the smell of an empty room
that has been closed for a long time.

You make me dwell
on things that are not good for me.

You try to keep me in your group
not talking to anyone,
as if I were in solitary confinement.
You make me talk to myself.

You may think that you are my friend
which you are not.
I choose to be around people
who keep you away.
Loneliness, you will not get me today.

—Rick Keller

MY VOICE

by Eli Mousavi, Iran
International Institute of Akron and Project Learn
Design by Daniel Cromaz, KSU Visual Communication Design student

MY VOICE

My voice is a boat that brought me
across a big sea.
My voice is a crib that holds me
as a child sleeps in her mother's skirt.
My voice is a shiny sea
where I swim into my real dream.
My voice is a rope with strong knots
that tie me to my past.
My voice is a key that opens a door
to a bigger world.

—Eli Mousavi

Credits

"A Winter Sunset" by Ted Kooser
First appeared in *River Styx*.
Used by permission of the author

"Vespertina Cognitio" by Natasha Trethewey
From *So Much Things to Say: 100 Calabash Poets*, edited by Kwame Dawes and
　　Colin Channer, 2010.
Used by permission of the author

"During a War" by Naomi Shihab Nye
From *You & Yours*, BOA Editions, 2005.
Used by permission of the author

"Driving while Black" by Mwatabu S. Okantah
From *Muntu Kuntu Energy: New and Selected Poetry*, Chatter House Press, 2013.
Used by permission of the author

"Soldier's Heart" by Maj Ragain
Used by permission of the author

"My Hero" by Billy Collins
From *Horoscopes for the Dead*, Random House, 2011.
Used by permission of the author

"Driving" by Kate Daniels
From *Three Syllables Describing Addiction*, Bull City Press, 2018.
Used by permission of the author

"My Mother's Name Lucha" by Juan Felipe Herrera
First appeared in the Academy of American Poets website, Poets.org.
Used by permission of the author

"How the Brain Works" by Maggie Anderson
From *Dear All,* Four Way Books, 2017.
Used by permission of Four Way Books.

"Fado" by Jane Hirshfield
From *The Beauty,* Knopf, 2015.
Used by permission of the author

"Testimonial" by Rita Dove
First published in *Poetry* magazine (Nr. 01/1998).
Reprinted, by permission of Rita Dove, from her *Collected Poems 1974–2004,*
    W. W. Norton & Company, 2016.

"Pescadero" by Mark Doty
First appeared in the *New Yorker* and *Deep Lane,* W. W. Norton & Company, 2015.
Used by permission of the author

"Moon in the Window" by Dorianne Laux
From *Facts About the Moon,* W. W. Norton & Company, 2005.
Used by permission of the author